The Power of Social Media

The Power of Social Media

IMPROVE YOUR KNOWLEDGE ON
SOCIAL MEDIA

Jim Stephens

CONTENTS

Introduction

Introduction

Do you own or operate your own website or online business? With the rising popularity of the internet, there is a good chance that you do. Whichever type of website you have, did you know that you could help to promote it with social media?

I'm sure many of you have heard of different social media sites like Facebook, YouTube, Twitter, MySpace, LinkedIn, Blogger, WordPress, and others. With a fairly large number of such social media websites having over a millions users, there is a good chance that by joining these sites, you not only make new friends but also find internet users that would be interested in visiting your website. Therefore, by joining these social media sites and then providing a link to your website in these sites, you should receive a number of new visitors to your website.

If you have totally no experience with social media or if you are still wondering how and why you should use social media to promote your website, then you may want to continue reading to find out more about the power of social media and how you can benefit from it.

1

∽

What is Social Media?

With the onset of many online business opportunities, which offer a chance for people to enjoy earning a living from the comforts of their own homes, more and more have become curious about what social media really is about, and how it can help their online business careers. First and foremost, social media can mean two things. For one, it can be a tool that is used for people to communicate and share certain things with their friends and love ones; and, it can be used as an internet marketing strategy that takes advantage of the influence of social networking sites like Facebook, YouTube, Twitter, MySpace, and many more.

When you get started with an online business, which is operated through your own web page, one of the things that you will need to attain in order to succeed is to drive a huge volume of traffic to it on a regular basis. Internet traffic simply means the number of people visiting your web portal; and, one of the best ways to do that is through the use of social media marketing.

One example of taking advantage of a social networking site to promote your website is by placing a link to it, directly on your Facebook account to be seen by others. Thus, if you have already done that, then you have already taken advantage of social media marketing.

One of the reasons why successful online marketers make use of social media to promote their online businesses is the fact that such websites are highly visited by millions of people on a regular basis. With Facebook alone, it actually has over 500 million registered users in a global scale. Thus, there is no question that a certain percentage of it belongs to your target market. Going back to that example, you are actually just taking advantage of one site; therefore, if you add the numbers of other powerful social media sites mentioned on top, then you may be able to have thousands of people visiting your site on a daily basis.

Social media is indeed one of the most powerful online marketing strategies that you can make use of, in order to gain more traffic to your site. However, you need to keep in mind that results from it may take time to get realized. This is because you will still have to build your reputation so that more and more people would follow your website. Always remember though that thousands of webmasters are able to gain success from it, and since they can, you should be able to derive the benefits from it as well.

To get started, it is best to know the types of social media marketing first. Aside from that, do not forget that most of these websites were not initially created for business purposes, but as a way to bridge gaps between people who are located far from each other. Thus, you need to build relationships first, as well as entertain questions from interested individuals from time to time.

2

~

Different Types of Social Media

If you are about to jumpstart your online business career with the creation of your own website, you should know that there are many online marketing strategies that you need to make use of, in order to gain success in it. One of which is social media marketing, and one of the things that you need to do to take advantage of it is to know its different types.

In general, there are two different types of social media namely off-site and on-site. By knowing the different types of social media marketing, you will be able to know the proper steps that you need to take in taking advantage of this online marketing technique. Aside from that, you will also understand better, why such steps are taken for the benefit of your own website.

Off-site social media marketing simply means the use of other websites, particularly social networking sites, in order to drive more traffic to your own website. Such websites would be the likes of

YouTube, Facebook, LinkedIn, MySpace, among others. Since these websites are being used by thousands, if not millions of users worldwide, they are great to take advantage of to drive more traffic to your site. Driving traffic to your site is actually one of the most important things that you need to achieve, in order to gain more profits from the products or services that you offer through it. With more people visiting your site, you will have more opportunities of exposing your products, and increase the chances of gaining profits from it.

Keep in mind that there are certain steps that you need to take in order to take full advantage of such websites. Aside from setting up an account properly in each of the websites you will make use of, you also need to come up with ways in order to have more people follow your posts, and the links that you would be placing on your account, which lead to the main site that you are conducting your online business on.

The second type of social media marketing as mentioned on top is On-site. Although you can already possibly gain more volume of traffic through your off-site social media marketing efforts, you need to make use of on-site solutions, in order to make sure that people stay long enough in your own website to check out what you have to offer to them. This would mean that you have to improve the kind of content that you have for your site, make use of certain techniques to gain your own brand identity, drive organic traffic from search engine, and such.

In a nutshell, these two types of social media marketing work hand in hand in gaining you more profits in your business. Thus, it is best that you make use of them both, so that you will be able to attain the success that you have been longing for.

3

⌘

How Can Social Media Benefit Your Business

Social media marketing is one of the top most online marketing strategies that internet marketers, and even local companies make use of today. This is because social media websites are being participated by millions of people globally today. In other words, whatever kind of niche you are involved with, you can be assured that a percentage of your target market is involved in these social networking sites. Thus, most likely, a lot of people whom you can consider to be your potential customers, are frequenting these social networking sites on a regular basis, and if you are able to get in contact with most of them, then you will have the chance of boosting your profits to a very high level.

If you are able to play your cards right, one of the benefits that your online business can derive from social media is exposure. In other words, if you are operating your online business through your own website, you can take advantage of social media marketing in order to gain huge volumes of traffic towards it. The more volume of targeted website traffic you can derive from websites like YouTube, Facebook, MySpace, and such, the more potential you have in increasing the number of sales for the products that you have on your web page.

You need to keep in mind though that most people who register to these social networking sites are those who want to get in touch and catch up with their friends and family. Aside from that, some also register with the hope of meeting that special someone who has been elusive all these years. Thus, before you introduce your business to them, you will need to build relationships first, in order to gain their trust. Aside from that, you should also build your reputation by getting involved with certain discussions and share important views about it, or by sharing certain contents found on your site, which may be helpful to people who belong to your target market. By doing that, people you constantly get in contact with through these social media platforms will soon anticipate more from you; and that is the proper time that you introduce your business to them.

Aside from driving more traffic to your site, once you have establish your online business to your peers on these social networking sites, another benefit you can derive from it is to acquire honest feedback about the products or services that you are currently offering. This way, you will be able to device certain strategies or modifications, in order to improve your business. Since the feedbacks you are receiving are provided by people who belong to your target market, you will be able to determine the proper steps to gain more success in your business.

These are just some of the benefits your business can derive from social media. Keep in mind that by getting involved with these social networking sites, it will also help you identify the needs of people within your target market. Thus, it will also help you not just in modifying your current product, but also possibly develop another product, which people will really appreciate and support.

4

~

Conclusion

In conclusion, you should now have a clearer picture of what social media is, what it can do, and how it can benefit you. As mentioned above, there are a number of different ways that you can use social media to promote your website. By remembering the above mentioned points and tips, you can definitely benefit from using social media to promote your website.

Therefore, start searching for social media sites you can use to promote your website or online business today and start using them. Soon, you will be able to see an increase in the number of visitors to your website and derive benefits such as more sales and money from this added traffic!